CONFESSIONS OF A NON-CONFORMIST

By Ed Byers

Confessions of a Non-Conformist

Copyright © 2010 by Edward H. Byers
All rights reserved.

Printed in the United States of America. No part of this book may be used or reproduced in any manner whatsoever without written permission except in the case of brief quotations embodied in critical articles and reviews.

Fifth Estate, Post Office Box 116,
Blountsville, AL 35031

First Edition
Cover Designed by An Quigley

Printed on acid-free paper
Library of Congress Control No: 2010925264
ISBN: 9781933580944

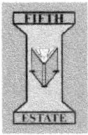

Fifth Estate, 2010

Table of Contents

A LOOK AT SOCIETY:

Confessions of a NonConformist	7
Finding a City's Soul: **Paved Streets or Dirt Roads**	9
Death of the Corporate Promise	13
A Reasonable Expectation of Race: **Defeating the Racists in Our Society**	18
Quiet Charity and Silent Grace	22
Professional Sport and Hero Worship: **Holding Athletes Accountable**	27
Giving Credit Where Credit is Due	31
False Patriots: **Why Eric Rudolph had to Face Justice**	35
The Redemption of Self	39
Questions of Violence in Our Society	42

A LOOK BEHIND THE BADGE:

Holding Someone Else's Angel: **A Lesson of Respect in Science**	46
A Lawman's Legacy	50

The Long Way Home	53
Driving While Black, Policing While Blue	58
The War on Drugs	62
An Open Letter to the Rookies	66
"Shots Fired!! Officer Down": When Our World Falls Apart	69
Law Enforcement's Defensive Tactics and Common Street Sense	72
Living in Defiance of Nature	75

A LOOK BENEATH THE BLACK BELT:

A White Man's Epiphany	80
The Faces Before Me	84
Legacies: Hoping for the Future While Remembering the Past	86
Satori and the Odd Kid Out	91
Enjoying the Present While Looking at the Future	95
That Kid	98

CONFESSIONS OF A NON-CONFORMIST

I am you, but not like you.

I am the gray man in a crowd, indistinguishable, always in the background. Take a second glance before you pass. Look closely at me. I see a distant fire, burning intensely at the fringes of awareness. I am engaged with you, perceptive to the feelings that burn within you. I share your intense personal experiences, sometimes not at my choosing. Look at the fire with me. See what I see.

I sense the powerful emotions of our shared human experience. I know that hurt can heal. It can lead to growth, pain can bring joy, and loss can lead to discovery. I have celebrated lives at the beginning. I have mourned lives at the end. I know the journey between to be the most important to our souls. It is never about the destination; it is always about the journey. Every step we take offers so much if we allow ourselves to be open to others and ourselves.

I do not believe that people stay the same. We are always growing, always changing. The self we defend, the public self, is nothing like the private self we keep carefully hidden. Occasionally, the private self reveals traits and characteristics we would prefer to hide. These brief glimpses in public burn like paper in a fire. I cannot turn away like most people. I am compelled to portray these feelings. These are the moments I try to capture in words; to sense the human experience at its basic level. If we do not learn from the experience; we fail to grow.

The human relationship is most powerful when shared, most crippling when hoarded. Only a non-conformist would embrace these very personal moments as a learning experience. To share these moments with you releases a heavy burden from me. These are the moments I try to capture in words; the human experience at its basic level.

A confession is admitting a role or responsibility. These are my emotions here, based on the actions of others. I have written my perceptions of their life experiences. To confess my role gives me the responsibility and ability to tell your stories.

And in the process, it sets me free……..

FINDING A CITY'S SOUL: PAVED STREETS OR DIRT ROADS?

Much has been written and said lately about the soul of the American city. "A world class city" or "cultural back country?" Among the chorus of loud voices, let me softly sing my version of that song.

I define a common soul as something from the past that projects into the future of a geographical area. The people, events, and circumstances of the past influence how we will act upon the issues which we confront today. And how we act today will determine how our children will act on the issues that affect their society in the future. The continuation of the values and morals from one generation to the next will fashion our human responses to social and environmental problems. In essence, that which makes us do what we do, is where our city's common soul lies.

The city's soul does not lie inside a speeding car on the interstate. You cannot hear it while you're on a cell phone on Martin Luther King Boulevard. Nor can you see it while dodging rush hour traffic on Main Street. You will not taste it in the fast-food restaurant where you will eat lunch. Nor will you experience it watching television from your comfortable living room. Chances are that you won't feel it while shopping at a mega-mall. It is there but well-hidden in those places. Like all good things, you have to search for it.

Inside the city, you may find it at a small, privately-owned business. The same place that you go when you want to be called by your name while you buy a used book or eat barbeque.

Maybe you'll catch a glimpse of a city's soul while it sits in a porch swing when the weather is nice, watching the neighbors walk by. You may see it drinking from a garden hose in the summer. Or, it may be helping a stranger fix a flat tire on the roadside, or perhaps holding a door open for the person behind you.

A large part of it is the plain everyday things that can be done in which a stranger says, "thank you." You may not see these things on the main roads in an American city but they're happening every minute in a neighborhood within the incorporated limits.

Those people who live outside the city limits have a clearer vision of the American city's suburban soul. And don't kid yourself; the two are connected like brother and sister. They may hate each other at times, but let nobody hurt one while the other is near.

Just outside the city's metro limits, you can find the region's soul around the town squares that dot the landscape. Listen to the stories while having coffee at the local drugstore or cafe. Open a soft drink at one of the small stores or firehouses and make new friends that resemble old faces you once knew. Re-ignite that feeling of community that may have faded within you. The embers and flames are still strong in these little towns, strong enough for you to carry home and pass on to your loved ones.

If you really want a dose of the flavor of an area, get off the paved road. Dirt roads are becoming scarce everywhere; you'd better enjoy one while you can. Talk to a local farmer and ask him about issues important to the area. I'll bet you can't see a farmer from your car; they don't work by the interstate since their farm was carved into off-ramps. Listen to what they say. I am always amazed at the wisdom that comes from people in overalls.

After you're done, take what you experienced and use it in your neighborhood. Teach your children about community, helping others, and sharing jobs and rewards. Show them that diversity is good and we can benefit from each other's strengths while we can rely on others to shore up our weaknesses. Reveal to them how civility to others fosters respect for all.

These types of lessons will make any American city a "World Class City" way beyond what London or Amsterdam could ever hope to be. And we can keep the American "Down Home Flavor" so important to most of us. Combine that with the promise of a clear blue sky and be thankful that an American city's soul goes back centuries.

Talk to the store owner, share a drink from a garden hose, or open a soft drink outside a country store and enjoy yourself. We have community riches beyond belief. They are not taxable and belong to all who care to preserve them.

Look for me on the dirt road, walking slowly.

DEATH OF THE CORPORATE PROMISE

If you are over forty, you watched your parents go to work every morning and come home in the evening. Day after day. Year after year. A couple of weeks off in the summer and a few days off close to the winter holidays perhaps, but the remaining time was spent faithfully in jobs that many of them would hold for thirty or forty years.

And when they reached retirement age, they were given a small party and some tokens of appreciation for devoting most of their adult lives to one company. But most importantly, they received a decent retirement income that would allow them to live comfortably in their remaining years. That was the corporate promise to our parents.

When we entered the working world, we felt this promise was still binding for us, too. We were told that if we were good workers, performed to the best of our abilities, and did what was "right," we would not only be assured of a job but would prosper in our working environment. Our employment would be as secure as our parent's jobs were. That was the corporate promise to us.

But the corporation has not been as faithful to us as it wanted its workers to be to it. Newspapers report mill closings and bank mergers weekly with footnotes of how many jobs are lost due to "streamlining," "outsourcing," or "downsizing." These are nice-sounding words that try to disguise the fact that your neighbors or relatives have lost their jobs - jobs that many have worked for the last twenty years.

There is a class of people that are especially hard hit; those workers over forty. Yeah, that's right, us. We saw the corporate promise that sustained our families and gave our parents a decent retirement. We were impressed. We had no reason not to be.

When I was in college, my career choices were geared toward government service, not corporate culture. My classmates were grooming themselves for corporate lives as engineers, pharmacists, and business managers. All of us felt that we were guaranteed jobs if we faithfully functioned. My salary potential was not as high as theirs, but I felt that my job satisfaction would compensate for the discrepancy. Time has shown that my job was considerably more secure than theirs.

As old college classmates do, we have kept in touch throughout the years. Nearly all of them have not found the corporate promise to be genuine. Indeed, most of them are disgusted with corporate America. One friend tells me that the pay ratio of workers-to-CEO in Japan is eight-to-one, while the same ratio in the United States is nearly one hundred-to-one. He tells me that in Japan, the average CEO makes approximately $200,000 per year.

According to a report published in *The Charlotte Observer* in 1997, the average American CEO makes almost $7.8 million per year when stock options and other perks are considered. That figure has grown since the report was published. Many American CEOs make the argument that they have risky jobs and deserve high compensation. I make the argument that they are eating their wounded by firing loyal workers. Try to remember the good managers in your work life. They showed respect, compassion, and encouraged their workers to grow. Today, most managers seem bent on making the bottom line better. That usually means management actions that put many older, higher-paid, loyal workers out on their bottom line - or the unemployment line, or the welfare line. The very dignities of these human beings suffer such severe blows that some never fully recover.

If a company is serious on making the bottom line better, it should concur with corporations in other countries and pay their CEOs less than the astronomical sums currently remitted to these inhibitors of Ivory Towers. Or Puzzle Palaces. Or Glass Houses.

The final call to action rests with us. Most of us hold stock in many of these companies. We need to make our feelings known to the Board of Directors. I believe that many letters stating dissatisfaction with CEO compensation would cause the Directors to make informed choices when they replace CEOs. Especially if the price of their stock begins to drop because we're selling it.

Obstinately, corporations ultimately deem themselves responsible to their shareholders. Plain observations reveal that they are more engrossed in profits than community welfare. We, the stockholders, should challenge a corporation's decision to close a small-town textile mill or a bank branch. The resulting employment changes affect our families and neighbors in manners that are rarely good. Tell the corporations that you are willing to suffer smaller stock proceeds to reinvest in companies that pay top management smaller, more reasonable, salaries. Make them see bleak future bottom lines as we make investments in their competitors.

I can think of nobody that cannot live on a couple of hundred thousand dollars per year in any American city. Even if they're the very best at what they do, cap their total compensation package at less than three hundred thousand per year. To pay more than that is morally bankrupt. Maybe the corporations won't get the well-known names or faces, but I'll bet there will be more than enough qualified applicants to pilot any business and continue to make it profitable. Many of those applicants could be those same neighbors or relatives that have worked so long at these companies. Such devotion, and inside knowledge of the business, makes sound management sense at any level.

It is funny in a karma-kind-of-way. We, the same people who have been "downsized", hold the ability to stop this mega-salary situation. Or in my common vocabulary, "fired."

Revenge *is* best when it is served cold.

A REASONABLE EXPECTATION OF RACE: DEFEATING THE RACISTS IN OUR SOCIETY

As much as it hurts us to admit it, different races possess different physical characteristics. Additionally, the cultural variations that exist between races within a society further the beliefs of some that we, as a people, are different. Racial tension, by its very definition, means different people pulling apart due to characteristics beyond their collective control. It is a tension created over perceived differences.

Some of us rely on our skin color as a defense for our own shortcomings. Or we use another person's skin tone as a justification of our own failures. It is a painless way to circumvent personal blame or responsibility. We find this is much easier than the difficult task of owning up personally for the responsibility of our actions. But, we need to do just that; stand up and take responsibility for our own actions. We need to call to notice the questionable actions of others, too.

Some members of our society find racial tensions to be fertile ground on which to breed hate and discontent. Often they shift their unwanted personal responsibility onto general racial or cultural hatred to justify their personal actions. These racists are from every ethnic group and preach that people can be categorized, hated, and hailed due to racial characteristics; characteristics that are beyond individual control. We need to stand up and advance the notion that individuals are responsible for their actions, not whole races of people.

Governmental programs have not been a success. By giving advantage to one race, they can force other persons to languish due to characteristics beyond their control. Preferred groups in hiring and other social programs will change after time. This decade's special group will be replaced by a new one when new statistical data and different immigration trends become apparent. The application of institutional remedies for social control has failed throughout history because they lack the soul of judgment.

The soul of judgment allows people to look beyond physical and cultural characteristics to judge a person by the most critical measure known; how that person treats other people. Many people have already stood for this principle, people from many races and of many colors.

No person should be scorned or saluted due to characteristics beyond their control. They should be judged on their personal responsibility toward others, regardless of the color of the person. That singular behavior has been, and will continue to be, the most important measure by which most people on earth should be judged. It is the true measure of a person. The tint of a person's skin or the culture they reflect does not bear on the fact that she or he can be totally unlikable; or conversely, a decent human being. We are not perfect creatures and, despite our best efforts, we retain the ability to dislike other people. If you must dislike someone, do so because they're a jerk, not because of the color of their skin. Do not let issues of race cloud issues of proper conduct. Hold all people of every color or culture to the same levels of personal responsibility.

A person's skin tone or eye shape should never define a social outcome or your personal perception of another human being. Make your judgments after you observe the person's actions. Hold everyone to the same levels of conduct. Do not let someone exhibit unacceptable behavior toward others, then excuse themselves by citing racial or cultural differences. Talk to the offending individual and make your convictions known. Compromise leading to understanding is crucial to lessening of tensions between the many different races in America. If enough of us stand up and call these issues to question, progress can slowly be made.

Individual efforts are the only way to rid our society of racism. Governmental and institutional efforts are feeble, ineffective attempts doomed to failure. Racists of all colors know this and frolic in this septic sea of ignorance. It is not a perfect world, but it is far better than it was thirty years ago. We have to collectively work toward future betterment. Progress has been made because some brave individuals stood up and made their respective stands.

The next time you hear a racist remark, stand up and make your feelings known about the personal responsibility of individuals. Remember, you're not alone. I'll stand beside you.

QUIET CHARITY AND SILENT GRACE:

An Open Letter to the present farmer and future developer of the field at any intersection outside the city limits.

Dear Sir or Madam,

I passed by your field a few weeks ago and saw that the "For Sale" sign had been changed to reflect "Sold." My initial feeling was of loss. I have only lived in the area for a couple of years, but I saw a small portion of why I moved here being taken away when I realized that the land would probably be subdivided and developed.

I know that you, as a farmer, can realize more profit in one year by selling the land to a developer than by farming it for another thirty years. I know that you, as a developer, can subdivide and build homes on the property and continue to employ others to make an income for your families. All of your reasons concerning the development of this land are valid, but I ask you briefly to consider mine.

People chose to live in an area for any number of reasons. My reason is that nebulous "quality of life" argument that never is the same for two people. That field I pass twice a day gives one of the best illustrations of the "quality of life" and I hope that my written efforts reflect my true feelings.

On occasions when my family passes your field and the crop isn't too high, we can see a flock of wild turkeys from the road. We, and other carloads of local folks, pull over and are treated to a rare show of one or two toms puffing and strutting while the hens appear nonchalant and continue to eat. The flock is healthy, probably due to periodic thinning by hunters. Once we watched for a full 45 minutes as the flock came within 15 feet of our truck. My children were just as thrilled as their parents to behold such a show. That show and how it affects all the people watching is the reason that I write.

In my hometown in rural southern Indiana, I grew up with two other boys that were as avid hunters as I was. Dickie, Steve, and I would leave school and immediately head for the fields or woods to hunt squirrels, quail, and cottontail rabbits. Of the three, I was the only one that had both parents; Dickie's dad had died in an auto accident before any of us could remember and Steve's dad had left his mother and their five kids. Steve worked at paying jobs a lot and never had the fashionable clothes or other items so desperately needed by teenagers. Nevertheless, he had two friends and a shotgun that his father had not taken with him. My friends and I learned many things during our long walks out of town on the railroad tracks. All three of us wanted jobs that allowed us to work in nature; Dickie wanted to be a farmer, Steve wanted to be a wildlife scientist, and I wanted to be a forest ranger. Steve and I would be roommates at Purdue University, knowing that our friendship would help us overcome future academic obstacles. Two of us made it to our chosen careers but the third was cut down as he entered the threshold of his adult life.

At the end of a hunting day, we would go to one of our houses and clean the game. Dickie and I knew that Steve depended on his rabbits and squirrels for more than just a hunter's pride of success. As we cleaned the game, more meat would be in Steve's pan of saltwater than in ours. Nothing would be said. Dickie and I would just put the meat there and Steve silently accepted it. It was offered with quiet charity and accepted with silent grace. We never directly talked about it between ourselves.

My dad, who had given me a magnificent Winchester 20 gage pump shotgun that he had purchased new, often chided me about coming home with only a couple of rabbits but minus ten shotgun shells. My marksmanship must not be as good as when I hunted with him, he would say. But one season I came home with six squirrel tails but only two skinned carcasses. He asked me if Steve had been hunting with me, smiled at my affirmative response, and patted me on the shoulder as he left the kitchen. He realized that his youngest son's aim was still true and his spirit was beginning to square as well.

One of our favorite fall hunting spots had four graves in a small overgrown glade of trees. The markers, mere creek stones, had various dates in the 1700's carved into them. We wondered what had happened to those early settlers and if anybody but us knew where the graves were located. As the markers needed cleaning each squirrel season, we realized that we were the sole caretakers of our remote cemetery. We took care of the graves and put wildflowers on them until our last fall hunting season, our senior year of high school. I didn't return until twenty years later.

Dickie became, and remains, a farmer. He endures hard labor and gains the self-respect that farmers know well. I became a National Park Ranger for ten years, but left after I felt I could no longer prostitute my convictions to remain loyal to politicians. Steve died in a motorcycle wreck after working a late shift at a convenience store our senior year. We never got to share that room in college...

Whenever I return home, I leave my family and walk to the town graveyard to visit Steve's grave. My eyes still tear over after all these years, evidence that I continue to grieve for my friend. During my 20th High School Reunion, I traveled to the old settler's graveyard and was amazed to see a subdivision of fashionable houses. The glade of trees was gone and a BMW coupe sat on the spot where the graves were, underneath a circular asphalt driveway. I elected to remain silent about the graves, it's probably best now.

I passed your field today and saw the sign again reflects "For Sale." I guess the sale must have not been completed. Regardless, with the current growth in our area, it will soon be sold. But I would ask that perhaps you make a codicil with the developer to build a third fewer houses than zoning allows. Have him charge a third more in price for each house. Use the space for greenways and woods so that the turkeys and other wildlife can stay. It could be named after something that was preserved rather than something that was obliterated.

Maybe your children or grandchildren could learn the lessons of quiet charity and silent grace the way that I did so many years ago. Better that than a paved-over past that will die with the memories of those that knew the area before it was developed.

Thank you for your time.

PROFESSIONAL SPORTS AND HERO WORSHIP:

HOLDING ATHLETES ACCOUNTABLE

Charlotte has an obsession to judge itself by the amount of professional sports that it can attract. Deliberations continue to bring a professional major league baseball team to join the Bobcats and Panthers. Some of us use the presence of professional sports teams to gauge our area's quality of life.

Coincidently, weekly stories appear about incidents where young, highly paid professional athletes are arrested while fighting in a bar. Or professional football players are found in a hotel room with four lines of cocaine and people of dubious character. Or professional baseball players are seen on national television spitting on an umpire or uttering racist statements. The Bobcats and the Panthers have players accused of drinking or dangerous driving. One former professional football player in Charlotte has been convicted of conspiracy for the murder of his pregnant girlfriend.

By nearly any rational standards, this is not behavior that we wish for our youths to imitate. I suspect that it is bad for the reputation of each club affected. Charlotte expects more of its highly paid, professional athletes.

I had only one sports hero; Steve Hamilton. He was never a household name but he was from my small hometown of Charlestown, Indiana. His mother remained there and died a couple of years ago. My mother and she remained close until Mrs. Hamiton died.

Steve was a relief pitcher for the New York Yankees in the early 1960s and I don't think professional athletes were paid nearly as much as they are now. Many pros had second jobs to support themselves and their families. Steve taught at Morehead State University during most of the year, but during the summer he did a magical transformation. Not only did he become a professional baseball player, he was from my small hometown.

On those hot and humid days, my friends and I would watch the Yankees and cheer when he would pitch. He was far more than just a New York Yankee during their heyday; he was someone that would visit our church with his mother. A real life hero that I could actually see! Heady stuff for a kid in his innocence in the mid 1960s.

During one hometown parade, Steve Hamilton was the guest of honor/grand marshal and rode in the back of a new Ford convertible. The whole town waved and yelled to him as he passed them. My older brother placed me on a certain street corner so I could get a good view of my hero. As he approached, Steve saw me holding my baseball glove. He reached down and held up a hardball and looked me right in the eye. I was stunned when he threw the ball directly at me. So stunned, that my brother later told me, that all I did was watch the ball as it sailed right past me and my friends quickly grabbed it. I could not move a muscle. My hero had looked right at me and made a personal connection that an eight-year-old boy could not comprehend. My buddies were elated that they had retrieved the ball, but I was heartbroken that I had missed it.

My brother left for a few minutes and returned with another hardball signed by Steve Hamilton. I can still recall the joy when he put that ball into my glove. My friends were envious; the ball he had thrown was not signed. How many millionaire ball players today would perform such a class act?

Steve died in 1996 after suffering from a terminal illness. I again was stunned; to me Steve Hamilton was still in his early 30s and wearing pinstripes. My hero, like myself, had aged. I had only recently come to the conclusion that I was aging. I had forgotten all those people from my childhood. Especially my heroes...

As Charlotte prepares to offer crucial concessions to lure a major league baseball team here, I believe that we must insist the players possess character and morals. I suggest an enforceable moral clause be inserted into each professional athlete's contract, similar to the ones used by sports equipment manufacturers seeking endorsements. If the athlete engages in public conduct that violates the clause, then they are terminated as members of the team and their future earnings are non-collectible. No arguments. No legal loopholes.

I do not follow the reasoning that they are "just young people growing up." Young people just out of college do not make salaries in the seven figures. Even the appearance of an improper action lessens their value as a public person. As we continue to make them the youngest millionaires, professional athletes must take responsibility for their actions. They need to realize the importance of being some kid's hero as opposed to some reporter's scoop.

My childhood hero touched me in a special way. If the truth was known, I bet that Steve Hamilton probably touched many people in his life. Students at Morehead State, kids hanging off the fence at many dugout doors, and other acts of grace and kindness that Steve did on a regular basis.

Like signing a baseball for a crying overweight eight year old boy from a small town.....

Godspeed, Steve.

GIVING CREDIT WHERE CREDIT IS DUE

Dear First Credit Card Systems,

Thank you for your generous offer to give a U.S. Soccer Platinum MasterCard to my daughter, Nichole. She was somewhat confused when she received your letter and she brought it to me. Nikki, as we call her, is only eight years old and not quite versed in the ways of personal finance. I assume that you obtained her name from a list of area youth soccer players, unaware of her age. Our conversation about the credit card, and her personal values, was enlightening. I thought you may find it educational.

Nikki's definition of a credit card was that "you can take it into stores and get stuff with it." She felt, after seeing her parents use one on increasingly rare occasions, that it was "a good thing." I explained that her perceptions were true, but that a bill for the purchases would be mailed at the end of each month. Upon receipt of the bill, if the total payment was not sent, interest would be added until the full amount was paid.

To explain it in terms she would understand, I made a play-purchase of toys valued at one hundred dollars. I explained that, if the bill was not paid within a short time, eventually the interest could become as much as the original price of the toys. After much intense concentration, she realized that the money used to pay interest could have been used to buy more toys.

I told her about friends who have been so deeply trapped in credit card debt that it took years to pay their balances. She questioned how your company could charge higher payments to people who could not pay the lower, original payments? She asked why your company thinks they could pay it later? Nikki also thought that it was unfair to make people pay a higher interest rate than the original, introductory, rate. I could not give her logical answers to her questions.

We decided to fill the application form to see if she qualified for the $100,000 credit line your company offered. Nikki has three dependents; a small box turtle, a mixed breed dog, and a domestic rabbit. She estimates that these dependents cost her about seventy dollars per year to support.

Nikki lists her occupation as "to learn at school." Her length of service at this current job is seven years, counting day care and preschool. Diplomas and certificates are available if you need them. She states that her employer will verify that she is a "well, good-learned, student." (I note that English continues to be an area of study for her.) She is apparently well-liked at this job as she visits her "co-workers" houses, spending the night regularly.

She is not rewarded with large wages. Nikki feels that her current occupation is a stepping stone to a future job that will pay much better. Her career goal is to work with ocean animals in their natural habitat. She realizes that she may have to remain in her current career for additional job training so her immediate goal is "to be good at learning."

To the best of her knowledge and understanding, she has no alimony, child support, or separate maintenance incomes to report. She is not in a "skilled trade, self-employed, or a professional." We feel she belongs in the "other" category.

She does not rent or own her residence. Her parents pay a mortgage (a type of credit that I did not explain at this time). Instead of rent, she has chores to do. These jobs include keeping the house clean, taking care of her animals, and taking care of her family members by "loving them and respecting them." She considers herself a vital part of the family. I know that her family members feel that she is a treasured member of that unit.

Nikki's assets are substantial. She has no checking or savings account, but she has seven dollars that she carries in a pouch. She also has a vast assortment of coins, foreign and domestic, hidden in her drawer for a total of $10.90. She values her stuffed animal collection at $80.00, the rabbit at $102, the dog at $103, and the turtle at $105. A collection of Dr. Seuss books is worth an additional twenty dollars. She has an old, tattered, baby blanket that she values at $199, however I feel that it is priceless. Her most precious asset is her family, which she values at "a billion dollars." Nikki's values remind me of what is truly important in life.

When asked what she owed, Nikki feels that she owes her family a large debt because they care for her, play with her, feed her, and give her shelter and love. Odd how sometime we adults overlook such important aspects of the things so close to us.

I told Nikki that you may not issue her the credit card. She said that "doesn't make her sad." Credit cards, she said, are probably "not a good thing" and should be avoided when possible. She is confident that her parents will take care of her. Money, she reminded me, is not important. Love and respect are two of the rarest riches any one of us could hope to possess.

I hope your company learns that someday.

FALSE PATRIOTS: WHY ERIC RUDOLPH HAD TO FACE JUSTICE

Members of the American patriot movement have come and gone. Federal agents combined with other officers continued their limited search of the North Carolina Mountains. That search has finally ended. In the hidden hollows and crooked trails of some of the most beautiful back-country in the eastern United States, these groups searched for an elusive prey. The members of these two dissimilar groups marched to different drumbeats; neither group heard the other's drummer. But America heard the drums beating loudly.

Many lives were interrupted in the search for one of America's most wanted individuals - Eric Rudolph. He was convicted of involvement in an abortion clinic bombing that left one police officer dead. A medical professional was maimed. Many other lives were permanently altered in this saga. Eric Rudolph's life while a fugitive was never calm or sedate. Every small-town corner, wooded hill, or city sidewalk held the unwanted threat of a confrontation with a law enforcement officer or bounty-hunter. That threat proved true over time.

Eric Rudolph stated that he bombed the abortion clinic to save unborn lives. Some people considered him a folk-hero for his flight to avoid judicial proceedings. A few of them called him a patriot for his actions. Other Americans felt somewhat differently and considered him a villain or a domestic terrorist.

American history supplies many examples of patriots. During the signing of the Declaration of Independence, John Hancock so proudly wrote his name in enlarged letters that the vision-impaired King of England would not require glasses to read the signature. Hancock was fully aware that the presence of his signature on a document of revolution could become his death warrant if his cause lost. However, he was willing to sacrifice his life for his political beliefs. Since then, the term "John Hancock" has been American slang for a proud signature.

A defining trait of a patriot is that person's determination to put his or her life in jeopardy to further their cause. American cemeteries are full of such patriots that paid the final price for our democracy. However, to take flight and hide after a decisive action is not the path of true patriots.

There are quiet patriots in every stretch of our country. They pay their taxes, vote their conscience, and make their sacrifices. Some even served in our country's wars and distinguished themselves with honor and bravery. They returned to take their rightful place among us. Although they may disagree with political issues, they will not take up arms against their government or fellow citizens. They show their dissatisfaction by taking an active role in the political processes to further their beliefs. They do not physically hurt their opponents. Their courage is evident in their commitment to our revolutionary, and peaceful, democracy. Part of our democracy is the American judicial system. It was enacted to protect persons and society while allowing individual rights and stopping unwanted sovereign interference. This system, considered revolutionary since its inception, remains one of the best in the world. Look in newspapers, the Internet, or on television to find stories of countries that fail to meet our judicial standards for its citizens.

Eric Rudolph faced the American judicial system and was convicted. Many people now view anti-abortionists with a less-than-sympathetic eye due to the bombing of clinics and resulting death and injuries. His actions of flight hurt, not helped, his cause. Both bombing and fleeing are too closely associated with cowards; people too false to be patriots.

Only in times of national conflict can bombing be sanctioned by the highest government in the land. It is taken against our enemies, not ourselves. Such actions are not for states, special interest groups, or private citizens to undertake. Our collective national honor will not permit our citizens to hurt other U.S. citizens. The Founding Fathers did not want it. We call it a felony.

Eric Rudolph did not meet the definition of a true patriot. His political cause suffered permanent damage due to his actions. His stated reasons of support for his cause did not outweigh the rights of others.

Listen now to the drums throughout the land, Eric Rudolph. The message that they send is not the one that your supporters want you to hear; your supporters are a very small minority in our vast democracy. Most people who support the right to life movement do not condone the killing of others. Your actions have hurt, not helped, your cause.

A political movement is only as noble as the courage and morality of its followers. Every day the manhunt continued, additional people forsook the very issue Rudolph held so crucial. The longer he remained hidden, public support grew weaker for his crusade. The longer he ran the more moral damage he did to his cause.

A true patriot would not do that.

THE REDEMPTION OF SELF

Loved ones or strangers, it does not make a difference. Relationships often fail and the pain is always internal. Some failed relationships cut like a razor; sharp, deep, and painful. Others eat away at our self-identity like a cancer; slowly dissolving our ability to care about ourselves. We build a protective shell around us by altering our social interactions with others. We hope the shell will protect us, but eventually it makes us isolated and alone.

The allocation of fault is human nature. It allows us to validate our perceptions of the failed relationship, even if those perceptions are not true. If we blame others, the validation falsely raises our self-righteousness. If we blame ourselves, we lower our self-esteem by suffering the personal pain of self-disclosure. We cannot see that blame is rarely the result of a single person's action. If we do not acknowledge our own contributions to the failed relationship, we hinder our ability to forgive and accept responsibility. By refusing to accept the personal burden of self-responsibility, the exercise becomes unrealistic and the results become unreasonable. We become confused and bitter, unable to continue life's journey. We self-arrest our spiritual and personal growth.

Mistakenly, we may believe that we grow stronger by suffering the pain of failed relationships. Actually the pain hinders our ability to have or develop other relationships. If we are fortunate, we move on quickly when a relationship sours. It is far better to leave with a few bruises to the ego rather than endure a crushing beating to our perception of self-worth. If we stay too long, the emotional devastation is so brutal that we forget to take care of ourselves. We forget the basic concept of self-help. Some of us allow this growing pain to continue until the consequences become headlines. These solitary few have lost the capacity to forgive – both others and themselves. They weep alone as the world cannot help them.

We lie to ourselves to ease our pain. We initially recognize the self-deceit, but over time we actually begin to believe the falsehood. As the deceit takes control of us, we become the very people we despise. Rarely asking for help, sometimes we spiral downwards into a dark, bleak, hole of self-loathing. A few of us cannot rise up again. Friends will offer help, but we rarely listen. Our preconceived notions are too dear to question, even at the risk of self-depreciation. The lie becomes too seductive, too alluring, not to believe. It can become a self-fulfilling prophecy.

Some of us give too much. We make sacrifices to our personal god of ego that we cannot afford. Everything we give to our perceived self robs us of a small portion of our soul. Like that cancer, this disease of self-deception creeps into our lives until we slowly succumb; too confused to determine the truth.

The most common danger is that we will not open our hearts when a genuine opportunity is there. We lack the self-esteem to take the risk. Good people will offer fulfilling relationships, but we will not recognize these honest opportunities. We are too weak and too hurt to try again. We will turn our backs and ponder what could have been. We will continue to suffer alone while help slowly drifts away.

We long for an honest relationship that provides love for what we are, not what someone else wants us to be. We want to be loved as the sinners we are, not the saints others wish us to be. If we are fortunate, we will find that fulfilling relationship. A pet, an infant, or perhaps another person will enter our lives. They will allow us to heal, to move forward again. The healing must start from within. We need, at the most basic level, a justification to be ourselves and nothing else. We seek a perfect love - to have a perfect trust.

A friend recently said that you must talk to the past to get to the future. The past may not answer. However, the silence allows us to express our hurt, forgive the transgressor, and move forward. And moving forward is the only way to the redemption of one's self.

The healing... and redemption... truly begins when we forgive ourselves.

THE QUESTIONS OF VIOLENCE IN OUR SOCIETY

Do you stop walking at the mall when you see a child being harshly punished by a parent? Or do you keep walking? What would you do if a teenage girl was being brutally beaten in a parking lot? Would you drive on? Would it make any difference if you knew her? What if she was your daughter or sister? What if she grew up to be your mother?

Many disturbing questions face our society when we discuss our collective views of violence. Our opinions about physical force are rarely in agreement. Pacifists condemn violence in all forms. Others support the use of force in varying circumstances. A few of us resort to force as a primary solution to problems. People display their destructive tendencies every day; they show no sign of fading away.

Police officers see the scared faces of violence every day. Cops mourn lost innocence when they respond to calls when parents have failed to control their rage. The faces of those children reflect confusion when their parents have hurt them. This bewilderment is more apparent than the hurt of the physical beating that initially brought law enforcement officers to their home.

Conversely, the police profession sometimes demands that force be used in the defense of life or limb. Some form of violence is allowed until the subject stops the behavior that made the individual officer respond with force in the first place. Any additional violent behavior after the subject submits is considered police brutality. Excessive police force should be reviewed given the officer's situation and the suspect's behavior, not a sterile office setting days later.

Martial arts instructors face different circumstances when they teach long-accepted responses to physical attacks. Many of these techniques terminate in broken bones or potential lethal blows or strikes. Once a violent attack is perceived, the student starts a series of responsive techniques. The sequence continues until the techniques have ended, disabling the attacker. The aggressor can experience permanent injuries for his or her aggressive efforts. Although it may sound extreme, such strategies enhance a student's chance of survival in the unforgiving streets.

Martial art students that have successfully repelled attackers state that they were acting automatically. They did not consciously understand what happened until the attacker was on the ground or retreating. Less fortunate students are dismayed when they cannot defend themselves on the street but constantly win tournaments. They have decided to be winners in artificial contests but failed to show similar resolve in an actual combat situation. In most street situations, a predetermined response to an attack might be the deciding factor between the two possible outcomes; victory or defeat. The great paradox of violence is that those people who continuously train in fighting techniques become people of peace. Survivors of violent confrontations do not feel the internal need for ego gratification in future conflicts. Martial artists know that force should be used as a last resort, only when retreat or common sense has failed. They know that the resulting harm to another person is not worth a temporary "lose of face" or a bruised ego.

How do we answer the questions of violence as individuals in a society? Do we allow others to hurt us or our loved ones due to a belief in pacifism? Or do we fight back for protection? What level of force is appropriate? Police research looks for quick cures every year. Officers use bean bags hurled from shotguns, aerosol agents that render attackers helpless, or electronic devices that put violent suspects on the ground with a touch of a button. None of these experiments have proven universally successful, or without risk.

Fewer solutions are available to the public. An unarmed tactic may not work against one person but may seriously injure another when applied by the same person. There is no way to tell the outcome of the techniques before applying them. There are no quick and reliable answers to violence.

And so it is with every individual in our society that faces a violent attack. Each person must decide when they will stop allowing themselves or their loved ones to be victims. This decision must be made with much thought and a crystal-clear view of consequences.

Perhaps gentle eye contact and a whispered "Slow down. I've been there" would be enough to stop the over-abusive parent in the mall. Dialing 911 on your cellular phone to report the assault on a city street may insure a police response. But what will happen in the minutes it takes the officer to respond?

And what if it's you? How will you answer the question of a violent attack against you or a loved one? Will you comply with an attacker's wishes while hoping for minimum injuries? Or will you fight back? Make your decision well-thought, with a clear mind, and before it happens to you. It will make your actions quicker and easier. You will need every advantage to survive intact, whatever your personal choice.

HOLDING SOMEONE ELSE'S ANGEL: A LESSON OF RESPECT IN SCIENCE

The weather is warmer and they will come, at least for another year. Theodore Roosevelt called them part of the "little forest folk" but I have never heard them called holy, until I met a Mountain Ute Native American named Don Whyte.

You are apt to see them while you're traveling 55 miles per hour on a paved secondary road in the Piedmont. Only when you're right on top of them will you recognize the shape of the box turtle trying to cross the road. If they're lucky and the timing is right, they'll make it ever *sooooo* slowly across the road and to their destination. Often we see them as road kill, silent testimony to the urban encroachment of our cities and towns into natural and rural areas. The turtles will not travel more than one mile from their birthplace, unless we decide to subdivide their ancestral home. Then they are forced to move on, to find a new home to lay eggs and seek out food. Forced to move to keep living.

Time is a relative issue between species. Some tortoises have lived to be over 100 years old. Most don't make it three years. They are tempting bite-size morsels to many other "forest folk." Even while in the egg, they are in jeopardy of being something else's lunch. As adults, many bear the mute marks of abuse from lawnmower blades, mischievous children, and dogs. Some even have fools' initials carved into their shells.

When I was a national park ranger, I had the fortune to work with Don Whyte. On paper, I was his supervisor, but in reality I learned much from this dedicated and gentle person. He had forgotten more about horses and mounted patrol than I would ever learn and I found him to be good company in all aspects of a ranger's work.

We worked in the desert area west of Tucson, Arizona. Among our duties was road patrol, performing traffic enforcement in a stretch of highway that was notorious in the national park system for motor vehicle accidents. We also had ongoing roles in wildlife research projects, particularly a study of endangered desert tortoises.

When we would find a tortoise, we would record as much data as possible to assist the researchers in their program. We recorded weight, the number of digits (toes), the location and time we found it, sex, and any numbers, telemetry device, or distinguishing marks on it. Determining sex was easy; red eyes were males and gold eyes were females. Once a rattlesnake researcher told us to turn a rattlesnake over and count its anal plates to determine sex. We determined that flipping a coin was far more prudent.

One day during traffic enforcement, Don and I found a tortoise trying to cross the busy highway. We pulled the marked police interceptor off the road and activated the overhead red and blue lights. We took the tortoise up a wash (small dry gorge) to complete the wildlife observation card. We dutifully measured, estimated weight, counted toes, and looked for distinguishing marks. As I was engrossed in converting pounds and ounces into grams, Don made an astonishing observation. Our topic of conversation during that patrol had centered on Native American religion. Don had explained to me that throughout the ordeals placed on Native Americans by the Europeans, they always managed to keep their religious beliefs. As this tortoise looked directly at me, Don remarked that turtles were generally thought to be representatives of the gods. I was stunned when I realized that I was holding someone else's angel. In one short afternoon, Don had given a sterile scientific project a soul and, in a very human way, reminded me why I became a national park ranger in the first place.

I spent the remainder of that season learning southwestern Native American lore from Don. He still serves as a national park ranger today. I know that Don, and others like him, will strive to do what's best for the parks, not what the National Park Service tells them to do. And that thought gives me great comfort...

During a lunchtime meeting this year, a friend stated that religion is not a substitute for faith; religion is a means to express one's personal faith and beliefs. We in the Bible Belt need to remember that we are not the only show in town. Tolerance and acceptance are essential so others may worship in a manner most meaningful to them, not necessarily to us. About 400 years ago, the Europeans came to America for precisely that reason - religious freedom.

When you see a box turtle trying to cross a busy country road, take time to help it. It is moving to keep living, maybe leaving a home now covered in cul-de-sacs. When all is said and done, the time you spend helping someone else's angel won't be deducted from your life. A title of one of Theodore Roosevelt books says it all, "Fear God, And Do Your Own Part."

A LAWMAN'S LEGACY

I suspect that parents don't spend as much time with their children as they want and I am no exception. As a parent of three, I appreciate the private talks with each and I wish they occurred more often. Driving back from town years ago, I asked my thirteen-year-old daughter if she had given any more thought to an occupation. She bluntly told me that she was thinking about becoming a cop.

My heart stopped.

I turned and looked at this beautiful young woman; the answer she had given me was not one that I wanted. She was a cheerleader at her middle school, blond with blue eyes, and the constant receiver of telephone calls from nervous young men. I was in my eighteenth year as a street-level Federal law enforcement officer, having served ten years as a uniformed National Park Ranger and the remainder as a plain-clothes Special Agent with the U.S. Customs Service. During that time, I had survived two shootings and seventeen additional incidents in which some level of force was needed to control a subject. At best, a cop's life can be perilous and the mean streets can be very unforgiving.

I explained to her that cops today are not as respected as they were twenty years ago due to some officer's misdeeds and, in rare instances, obvious criminal behavior. More agencies require a four-year college degree each year. The pay, I told her, is minimal for that level of education. Most officers have to work another part-time job to make financial commitments and give their families a decent quality of life. The stress is dreadful and many of us turn to undesirable behavior to escape the terrible scenes that we are required to witness each shift. Alcoholism, divorce, and early heart attacks seem to occur more in a cop's life than that of an average citizen.

She replied that she respected the school resource officers at her school. Those county deputies were polite and genuinely wanted to help people. The desire to help people, she said, was the principal reason behind this career choice.

She made me think about my reasons for entering law enforcement years ago. I remembered all of the fine and honest officers that I had worked with over the years. From small town marshals driving decrepit cars, tradition-bound Texas Rangers on horseback, starched state troopers in shiny interceptors, farm-raised deputy sheriffs in four-wheel drive trucks, high-tech Federal agents, and aggressive Assistant United States Attorneys; they shared that common goal - to help other people. Often the victims of a crime cannot help themselves and their silent pleas are visible on their faces when they are interviewed by officers. I came to understand that the basic desire to help others is the common factor within each of these cops; it was in them before they pinned their shield or star on their chest. It was not something that they learned in college or at a basic police academy.

My heart started again.

There came a time when I had to let each of my children go. They left our home to pursue their careers and add further chapters to their lives. Whatever they chose to do with their lives, I hope that they perform it to the best of their abilities.

Should my daughter become a cop, I know that she is doing it for the right reason; to help other people. I hope that is the legacy that I have given her. If she graduates with a degree in criminal justice or completes a basic law enforcement academy, I will also buy her the best body armor on the market. At best, a cop's life is perilous and the mean streets can be very unforgiving.

THE LONG WAY HOME

For two Federal agents trapped in another city by a snowstorm, the hotel was a good place to spend the night. About fifteen other people ate their dinners around us in the bar. Doc and I sat alone, content to have a nice place to stay overnight.

Doc was a Navy Corpsman who was assigned to the Marine Corps. He saw combat during the first Gulf War. He then joined the New York City Police Department at a young age. He rose to the rank of Detective and worked a Gang Unit before being hired by the U.S. Department of Homeland Security. We both live in North Carolina now. I knew Doc for over eight months before we had our first assignment together this night. He is my idea of a typical New York City Cop. Gruff, blunt, and built like a fireplug; he has an opinion on any subject. He was a good partner and pleasant company this cold winter night.

We talked about our old jobs. When I asked Doc if he missed New York City, his short reply was, "No. You have no idea what it was like for me there."

On September 11, 2001, Doc responded to the terrorist attacks at the World Trade Center. He, and the other surviving responders, felt helpless to the destruction around them. As his prior Navy training was in medical care, he was immediately assigned to the City Morgue. He spent most of the next six months there, separating bodies and body parts from physical property and evidence. He would tag everything in zip-lock bags.

After one grueling thirty-day stint, Doc was told to return to his borough and answer the Detective Squad's telephone calls. He was to complete a form to document the information received in hopes that someday the Department could resume normal police work. Doc couldn't take any time off; the city needed every cop. Needing a break from the morgue, he gladly accepted the one-day assignment. It would provide some temporary relief from the carnage.

After about two hours of routine telephone calls, Doc began receiving public inquires and radio calls about an aircraft crash near his station. He grabbed a car and sped to the scene. After many weeks of immersion in dead bodies and body parts, he felt an overwhelming desire to help someone. Anyone that was living, rather than dead.

When Doc arrived at the crash site, many houses and the aircraft were still in flames. Chaos prevailed as it always does during the first critical minutes of an emergency. He ran towards a group of familiar faces; his sergeant, lieutenant, and captain were standing in a group. As he started to go into the crash scene, he was admonished to stay out until others arrived to help.

Doc's New York temper took control and he cursed them. He called them cowards, too afraid to help the injured. Doc charged towards the cries for help. To stop him, his sergeant grabbed his shirt but Doc continued into the heart of the crash scene. He dragged his supervisor over a block until the man let go of his shirt and ran alongside him into the flames.

As they entered the heart of the scene, a dazed man came out into the street and motioned for their help. "They're in my back yard," he kept repeating. Doc and his sergeant ran around the side of the house. They found part of the passenger cabin with twelve people still strapped into their seats. All of them were obviously dead. The pattern repeated itself throughout the evening and the officers were confined to interviewing witnesses. Doc would find no rescues to be done that night.

Doc was immediately sent back to the City Morgue to assist with this latest batch of bodies. As the ambulances backed up to the doors, body fluids would seep out the rear doors and onto the bumpers. Many of the crash victims were brought to him in large buckets. He did well until he started working on his second child, and then the grief was overwhelming. He could not continue.

Like many other New York City responders to both disasters, Doc went through counseling per order of the Police Department. Cops are bright; they know what to say and what not to say. Doc was released from counseling. He later took the position with Homeland Security, eventually moving to Charlotte.

I asked Doc which was worse, the World Trade Centers or the aircraft crash full of people returning home to the Dominican Republic. Doc looked up for a moment and his eyes clouded. Then, for the first time, I saw a New Yorker that did not have anything to say. After a moment's silence, he silently shook his head no and did not say anything. He did not want to continue the conversation. I believe that, for the moment, he was back at the New York City Morgue, reliving his personal Hell in a city he had left behind.

Although they may not speak with counselors, cops are bright. They will wait until they can speak with another cop, someone who walks in the same world and intimately knows their problems. They will slowly work through their demons with friends who understand and empathize. Friends who will help them face their horrifying secrets. It may take many conversations with many cops over a period of time. Cops will show their brothers and sisters how to find solace in the everyday rough moments of life. They will show them how to function again. Cops trust that their friends will help them find their way back and show them their way home again.

The rest of our conversation that night was about Charlotte and making a home in this southern city. Doc likes Charlotte with its friendly people and smaller-city atmosphere. The lower cost of living and temperate weather is nice, too. He likes most of our partners and is anxious to move ahead with this life, far removed from New York City.

The next day we returned to Charlotte and shook hands outside the airport. Doc was on the telephone, talking to a friend in New York City who was caring for his dog. The dog was sick and he was asking his friend to take the animal to a vet for x-rays. He was worried about his canine friend and the compassion in his voice was obvious. I knew he had a full day ahead of him. He was still looking for a house and wanted to look at some new cars that evening. But his dog was ill and his first priority. Doc was solving the problems of everyday life at his new home in Charlotte, North Carolina.

Welcome home, Doc. Welcome home.

DRIVING WHILE BLACK, POLICING WHILE BLUE

A current complaint against police officers is that skin color determines an enforcement action. Some members of the public believe that issuances of violation notices are racially motivated. Traffic stops, they continue, are determined by the ethnicity of the vehicle's occupants.

In North Carolina, the State Highway Patrol has become the latest target of these allegations. The Patrol is a proud organization, built on honor and shaped by prestige. As a state agency, the troopers are not fond of defending themselves. They quietly endure the criticism, showing a refinement that exceeds normal etiquette.

During traffic stops, it is nearly impossible to determine the ethnicity of a vehicle's occupants during movement. In ideal conditions, many tasks must be successfully completed before the trooper steps out of his or her car. When Doppler radar is used to determine that a vehicle is speeding, the trooper must compare the displayed target speed with observations of which car is traveling at a higher rate than adjacent traffic. This observation is normally made at distances exceeding one quarter of a mile.

The trooper then locks in the radar's display, maneuvers the police car to turn around, and maintains visual contact with the target car. If the car leaves the trooper's sight, then no violation notice can be given. At 65 miles per hour, the trooper must control the police car and turn in the median, then enter opposing high-speed traffic to start the pursuit.

As the trooper catches up with the target vehicle, he or she must key the plates into a mobile computer terminal or operate a radio. This is done to give the officer advanced notice of any dangerous situations. It also serves as an attempt to identify the driver later, should something go terribly wrong.

The trooper then decides the best possible place to make the stop. And the driver never cooperates, always pulling past the desired spot to one with a more hazardous exposure to high-speed traffic or a steeper grade. The trooper's approach and strategy must change with the location to ensure everyone's safety.

After the target car has stopped, the trooper places the police car behind the citizen. A quick inspection of the car's condition is done to note anything out of the ordinary. Then the trooper begins a measured approach to the car. At this point, after the car has been stopped, the trooper takes his or her first intensive look inside the car. Hand position, occupant gestures, and nonverbal communication cues are noted before the trooper speaks.

Normally, it is during this interior inspection that the trooper discovers who is inside the target car. Many steps are completed before ethnicity is known.

Now multiply the many different factors that come into play. Tinted windows, graphics on the windows, and vehicle height are physical factors that can obscure a vehicle's occupants. Mental factors, such as driving while intoxicated, a felon fleeing from a just-committed offense that has yet to be reported, or a fugitive from an ancient crime that believes his time is finally up, can also turn a trooper's routine traffic stop into a dangerous predicament. These are far more important to the trooper than the color of one's skin.

I would not ask you to believe me. Try it yourself. Pick a clear day, and then choose a speeding car coming in your direction. Can you tell what color the driver is before it passes you? Probably not, especially if you factor in the additional tasks noted above. Good luck trying to define a driver by the type of car, too. That is the quickest way to disprove personal biases, as I am sure you'll find out when you try it. You'll soon learn that the only colors used in traffic stops include blue and red when describing the color of the target car.

The key factor for any officer to observe in a traffic stop is public safety. Then, in a close second, is officer safety. All other considerations become distant thirds. The desire to stop drunk drivers, speeders, and reckless drivers is a goal that we, as a society, want our troopers to accomplish. We have not told them to only stop drivers of a certain color and let others go. That would not accomplish their task of keeping the public safe. We ask no less of that from them.

I don't know any trooper that cares what color your skin is, but they're quick to note the color of your car if you're speeding. We should allow the troopers to continue to perform unbiased law enforcement on our state roads. My personal observations had not led me to believe that they're doing anything other than just that. The Patrol deserves our full support. We should give them no less.

THE WAR ON DRUGS

A United States Border Patrol Agent lost his life in the summer of 1997, near a dusty southern Arizona border town called Nogales. He was a naturalized U.S. citizen, an immigrant from the Ukraine who devoted, and lost, his life in service to his new country.

This shiny-faced new agent hadn't been out of the academy for more than a year. He and his partner tried to interdict a group of foot smugglers carrying marijuana. Using border law enforcement slang, "they jumped some mules hoofing mota through the brush." The agent tried to arrest the suspects using accepted arrest techniques ("He tried to prone them out") and his partner was coming to his aid to assist ("Going to give him back up"). One suspect started to struggle ("He went squirrly") and the agent attempted to gain a more secure posture ("Tried to cuff him"). One of the remaining suspects pulled a weapon from under his shirt ("The other mope drew") and discharged the weapon ("He popped a cap"). The agent was shot point-blank in the head and died.

The individual parts to this tragedy happen so often on the southwest border that slang actually exists to describe the incidents. Since the death of this Border Patrol Agent, more have been shot and killed. One was the first female agent killed wearing the green uniform of the U.S. Border Patrol. A dubious honor, at best.

Nogales, Arizona, and the surrounding areas would not seem like America to you. Culturally, it's hard to tell the difference between America and Mexico in those parts. Sometimes the international fence, where it's up, might give you a geographical clue. However the manners, customs, and people are virtually interchangeable in the small towns on both sides of the border. Spanish is the primary language and English is a secondary type of communication. Cinco de Mayo is a far larger celebration than the Fourth of July.

Neither Nogales, nor Mexico, is bad. Most of the people there are hardworking, family oriented, and friendly to a fault. The major problem is simply money. The very few decent paying jobs are quickly and permanently filled. Most Americans make more in two months than most Mexicans make in a year. Some border villages lack adequate water or sewer systems. Mexico is not too concerned about the AIDS outbreak; more Mexicans die of simple dysentery in a day than Americans succumb to AIDS in the same period.

Take that poverty living so close to American prosperity and add a well-funded international narcotics smuggling organization. It does not take much insight to know what will happen. Top off the mixture with a liberal dose of arid mountainous desert and sprinkle in under-gunned law enforcement officers and agents. The mix then becomes explosive. Only by common sense and good grace do deaths not happen more frequently.

The desert is cold at night. Nighttime surveillance plays tricks with overworked eyes, making trees dance and shadows float. It's hard to tell your best friend from six feet, but trees fifty yards away glow absurdly in the moonlight. Sound is amplified over great distances and the horrible sound of a stray gunshot is impossible to pinpoint until daylight. And daylight seems to take forever when you hope the gunshots will not happen again.

Can you imagine how a kid from the Midwest could perform in such an environment? Then imagine how hard it was for a Ukrainian immigrant to adjust to the same conditions. Coming from a former Communist country, he probably wanted to treat aliens with some measure of dignity. Good officers always do.

Senior Trooper Robert Dent of the Oregon State Police said: "Law enforcement is where you get the test before you get the lesson." The lessons of border narcotics interdiction are plenty and always dynamic. The consequences of most tests in law enforcement are not so severe. You learn from your mistakes and try not to misjudge again. Here, the test occurred before the lesson could be learned by this new agent. He did the best he could at the time, but it was not good enough to pass the test. No blame offered here, just an observation.

The lessons are learned every day by officers and agents working worldwide in the War on Drugs. Unfortunately, a few of them will only take the test. Most officers won't take the final exam so early in their education. Their remaining friends will learn their fallen buddy's lesson and continue with their jobs - hopefully a little wiser and a lot more cautious.

Americans will read of their sacrifices and turn the page. Memorial services will try to offer closure to the living. But to a Ukrainian immigrant who gave it his all while trying to protect the borders of his adopted country, "Vaya con Dios, mi compadre."

His name was Alexander Kirpnick and he worked for the Nogales District of the United States Border Patrol. Think about his lessons in courage, self-sacrifice, and patriotism the next time you debate the War on Drugs in your far away home.

AN OPEN LETTER TO THE ROOKIES

Glad to see you made it through the basic academy. It was nothing compared to real-life on the streets. You look pretty proud of yourself right now. Give me a few minutes for some honest talk before you go into those streets. I have thirty years of experience as a street cop. I want to tell you a few things; listen to my experience.

That handgun on your hip only weighs about eight pounds but remember that its role is the heaviest that you'll carry for the next twenty-five years. It has only one function, to fulfill an instant task that society trusts to no other of its members. When it comes out of the holster, be sure that you completely understand the ramifications of what you're about to do. Also understand the ramifications to yourself, fellow officers, and the public if you fail to act. Confused? You should be. There is no finer line that I know of in any job or occupation.

Learn how to use your baton. You will be involved in many situations where lethal force will not be justified and pepper spray will not be effective. You'll need some level of force to complete the arrest. Unless you've studied the martial arts for a long time, your baton will be your best bet. Don't leave it in the car.

Your badge shines for a reason. Keep your behavior sterling; so you don't tarnish it. People will watch your every move; on or off-duty. We can't make the small mistakes that most people make and expect to be forgiven. Some people will respect you just because you wear that badge, but that kind of respect can be quickly lost. True respect must be constantly earned. Never forget that.

Many younger members of society will see you as a role-model. Some of them don't have much else to use for comparison, just cops and crooks. Take time to talk to the kids over ice cream, or shared candy. Just a quiet moment of genuine concern may be enough to encourage them to stay straight. Used correctly, this may be a more powerful weapon than your handgun, but that's only me thinking out loud.

Speaking of which, your mind and voice will be your most used tool while you're on-duty. Sometimes it is best to let a citizen vent to retain their dignity; other times you'll want to verbally control the situation before it escalates into a physical confrontation. Watch the cops that you admire and see how they operate. See what works for a seasoned officer and use it to your advantage. Most good cops would rather talk than fight. There are people on the street that you cannot physically subdue and it will get worse with age. Youth, with attending quickness and strength, is fleeting. You will grow old. Look at me.

Get a hobby or interest outside of this job. Keeping in touch with people that are not cops will give you a base of reality that some of us don't have. Remember that cops tend to group together and sometimes you'll want a fresh or different perspective on an issue. Hard to get that when you're at a role call.

Don't be in such a hurry to promote up the ranks. Good street cops are hard to find and good supervisors even harder. Put in your street-time and don't pursue the desk job in the first part of your career. It's not why you hired on in the first place. The citizens, and us, need you. Make that difference, I believe you can. I have faith in each of you.

You may not like some of us and we may not like some of you, but we're family now. I may not share a cup of coffee with you but if you need help, I'll risk my life and defy the laws of gravity to get to you. I expect the same from you. To have it any other way means that the thin blue line of justice will crumble. Do your part to keep it strong. I have. That's my legacy to you.

Have a safe shift.

"SHOTS FIRED!! OFFICER DOWN":
WHEN OUR WORLD FALLS APART

You have no idea what it's like. Our friends we had lunch with are now fighting for their lives on a greasy street or dark alley. Acquaintances that we care about are face-down with life-threatening injuries. People that we spent time with on fishing trips or around a barbeque in our backyards cannot respond to our frantic radio calls. We rush to find them, to help them.

Seconds become hours when nobody is there to stop their bleeding or give them shelter from those who hurt them in the first place. Chances are they didn't even know their assailants before the incident started. If they had known them, they would have called more of us to help. Nobody would face such savage animals alone.

We're not there to hurt anyone; our goal is to help. Sometimes you ask us to put our safety on the line; and we do so without hesitation. If our training works and our split-second judgments are correct, we can escape an encounter with no injuries to ourselves and little or no injuries to our prisoners. Even though that is what you expect of us, you rarely give us praise. Often the results are not optimal. We survive a deadly encounter to find ourselves crucified in the newspaper and television. We get administrative time off to "help our healing process" but you suspect it is because we're lunatic killers behind a badge. Nothing could be farther from the truth.

We deliberately put ourselves into harm's way like no other public servants. Firefighters, paramedics, and public service employees can analyze their opponents and take time to implement measures to enhance their safety. We're never quite sure what to expect and usually don't have time to make every safety requirement possible. Often, we're alone and the danger becomes real in an instant. When the moment of truth comes, we can never be too prepared. Law enforcement has been called hours of sheer boredom punctuated by seconds of sheer terror. How very true it is.

For the next couple of days, we will wear black ribbons around our badges as a public sign of mourning. We will hear the bittersweet sounds of Scottish bagpipes at the memorial service and tears will crowd our vision. But we'll be back for our next shift, dealing with all the uncertainties again. We are your protectors. You'll see us and not know what to say. Some of you will offer your condolences, but most will try to ignore the issue and tell us to have a nice day. Nice days are for fishing trips with our friends and backyard barbeques with our acquaintances. Not for walking on a greasy street and down a dark alley. Tell us something that really matters for us. Tell us to have a "safe shift."

And give us the respect that we're due...

LAW ENFORCEMENT'S DEFENSIVE TACTICS AND COMMON STREET SENSE

Have you ever wondered what cops learn when they are practicing arrest techniques, especially when a supervisor is not present? Shhhh....here's a quick peak:

<u>Talk nice. Think mean.</u> Always treat your suspect with courtesy and respect while thinking of how you will defend yourself if they attack you. When the attack comes, you will be better able to react.

<u>Keep your suspect's hands visible.</u> The eyes may be "the windows to the soul" but it is the hands that will hurt you. Knives, small handguns, needles, and clubs are easily hidden by the hands and your suspect's body. Make the suspect show you both sides of his or her hands at the onset of your contact.

<u>Stay out of the suspect's danger zone.</u> It can take up to a full second to react to any unanticipated attack. That is too long for many people to recover and mount a defense. Stay up to eight feet away from unarmed suspects. Stay at least 21 feet away from suspects armed with an edged weapon or a knife. Use cover first, then concealment if no cover exists. Approach suspects from the rear, not the front, if possible.

Handcuff first, and then search thoroughly. If you feel a suspect may have a weapon or are unsure, handcuff them before searching. Officer safety and public safety are always valid reasons to temporarily apply handcuffs. Always search the area where the handcuffed hands can reach first, then the entire body afterwards.

Never underestimate your suspect. Cute little kids can become cute little killers in a heartbeat. Always assume that an attack is eminent and prepare your response appropriately. Firefighters call it "preplanning" and do it on a regular basis. Having a response already in mind adds critical seconds in your favor during a critical incident.

Guns do not always stop adversaries. Many cops and crooks have continued to return fire after receiving fatal gunshot wounds. With the exception of wounds to the brain, the body does not abruptly stop all actions when it is hurt. As a general rule, smaller caliber weapons take longer to stop suspects. Shot placement and multiple shots become very important with 9mm and smaller calibers.

Continue to fight until the suspect is handcuffed or neutralized. DO NOT GIVE UP! Your mind is your most important tool in police work. It is also your most important survival weapon. Keep in mind that YOU WILL SUCCEED in this confrontation and continue to fight until your adversary is in custody or cannot continue to hurt you.

Wear your body armor whenever you can. Some of the functions of a cop make it impossible to wear body armor every day. However, when you suspect that something could go wrong, are anticipating any enforcement action, or performing patrol duties, wearing your body armor makes good sense.

Always use cover and back-up. No incident is worth your life. No matter how much we plan an enforcement action, the unexpected always happens. Be realistic when assessing changes. If there are too many crooks or a poor location, do not take action until more help arrives. It is always better to let the violator go and have another cop back you up a couple of miles down the road. No load or bust is worth your life.

Remember the First Rule of Law Enforcement. Always come home. Somebody, somewhere, cares about you. Do not make the rest of their life difficult because of a careless mistake. Make your chosen work as safe as possible.

LIVING IN DEFIANCE OF NATURE

Mankind cannot continue to live in defiance of nature. We, and our children, pay terrible prices for our arrogance. Our best, and worse, intentions haunt us in unforeseen and terrible ways.

In 1988, the National Park Service assigned me to the now-famous Yellowstone fires. Rangers from nearly every government level were urgently needed. I was flown from Tucson, Arizona to Phoenix, where we picked up additional Federal rangers that would assist in firefighting efforts. As we lifted up from Phoenix's SkyHarbor Airport, we could see the fire plume in the distance. It was unsettling to see a convection smoke column from a forest fire that was 600 miles away.

The ever growing firefighting force included college students, volunteers, prisoners, and temporary help. Due to jurisdictional concerns, nearly all of the responding National Park Rangers were assigned to security. We patrolled the main fire camps, which became small cities in a matter of days. Additionally, we were helicoptered to camps in the remote back country to provide security for sleeping firefighters and food supplies from displaced grizzly bears. Working in pairs, the Rangers patrolled the camp's perimeter at night. At dawn, we patrolled farther out. One morning, we observed where a large grizzly had scraped a tree near the camp. The marks were at least twelve feet up the trunk and the bear had left a massive paw print in the soft earth. Our four hands could not cover the track. My partner patted her .357 Magnum revolver and said, "Not enough gun!" Quite the understatement considering the physical signs we had discovered. I had a small knot in my stomach.

The first few days of the fire were surreal. Large grizzly bears, moose, and bison were displaced from the fire and readily observable as they sought safety. The only safe havens were the mountain meadows where we based our camps. Many of these animals wandered into the helipad at the Fan Fire, where my partner and I were assigned one afternoon. Firefighters and Rangers would stop by the helipads to see the different types of aircraft and watch the wildlife. The public also stopped to watch flight operations.

As the sun was setting at the helipad, a nearby ridge literally exploded in what is called a "jackpot." This is a quick, nearly spontaneous, combustion of trees. Whole ponderosa pines burned in as little as five seconds. All creatures present, including the omnipresent grizzlies, turned to watch the fire advance. By then, I had spent 12 years as a Ranger and fought many fires. I had never seen such a display of fire and its energy. The fire raced at speeds that most four-wheel-drives couldn't obtain that quickly. The Fire Boss/Incident Commander of the Fan Fire, a veteran Federal firefighter with nearly 30 years on the job, was standing next to us. He let out a sigh, turned to us, and confided that there was no way these fires could be extinguished until winter came. The knot in my stomach grew as I realized he was right. Months later, after the first snow, the fires were officially considered "controlled."

The National Park Service had defied nature in Yellowstone National Park. Fire, an important part of the natural environment in the West, had been suppressed for over 150 years. The fuel buildup was incredible and foolishly ignored. Eventually, nature solved the problem and the resulting fires taught me that no matter how hard we try, we can never fully control nature. Yellowstone is recovering to its natural state and the stewards of our public land learned a valuable lesson in fire management versus fire suppression.

During September of 1999, I met people that had the same knot in their stomachs that I experienced 11 years ago in Yellowstone. Eastern North Carolina had been battered by a hurricane and subsequent flooding. Their losses were huge; they now know the terrible cost of living in defiance of nature. They came to the same conclusion that I made that day at the Fan Fire Helipad, that nature cannot be fully controlled.

Nor should it be. Mankind has to accept that they are a part of the ecosystem, not the masters of it. Every forest or field that we pave over becomes another nail into our own environmental coffin. As our natural world changes ever so slightly with each disturbance, the cumulative effect becomes a sword hanging over our heads. We have to learn to live in harmony with our natural world, not in spite of it.

As the residents of eastern North Carolina rebuilt their lives, let us hope that they built their houses outside the flood plains or away from the barrier islands. The recent flood was called a 500-year flood, which means that one of this magnitude only comes every 500 years. I have yet to hear anyone mention that a 1,000 or a 10,000-year flood is also possible. Weather, as we learn again, comes in groups. It could be 500 years or it could be in five years, but the floods will come again. As will major hurricanes with their devastating winds.

Far too many of us will ignore nature's warnings. We will become victims to be interviewed as we wonder aloud how we'll rebuild our homes that have been flooded or blown away. The artifacts of our lives will be committed to the moving winds and waters. We'll have an empty feeling in our stomach as we question why it happened.

Some of us will learn. We will have that knot in our stomach and the awe will be seared into our memories. We will build homes that blend with the environment, rather than structures that defy it. Buildings will be made with special construction techniques to enhance survivability. We will choose our building sites with consideration of the land, rather than using riskier sites that afford a better view or higher social status. We will try to live in harmony with nature.

A Cree Indian prophecy knew this well: "Only after the last tree has been cut down, only after the last river has been poisoned, only after the last fish has been caught, only then will you find that money cannot be eaten."

A WHITE MAN'S EPIPHANY

Like a stubborn skin rash, race relations in the world erupt to the surface periodically. People blame others of a different skin tone for their personal troubles or professional difficulties. Theoretic arguments involving events that happened years ago (sometimes literally hundreds of years ago) are presented as if the offending actions happened yesterday. The ultimate responsibility of bringing slaves to the new world or the state of current events if the South had won the Civil War is far too complex for my simple mind. I find the arguments academic since the outcomes were determined before I was born.

So it pleases me to leave this confusing world a few times a week by dressing in a white judogi (judo uniform), tying a black belt around my growing waist, and bowing into a dojo (place of enlightenment) to practice the martial art of Judo.

Judo ("The Yielding or Gentle Way") was founded by Dr. Jigaro Kano in Tokyo in 1882 after he studied many forms of jujitsu (techniques of flexible responses during unarmed combat). Kano, a noted educator, saw that his countrymen were restless after the fall of the feudal system so he perfected different jujitsu techniques into judo to give them direction. The suffix of "do" means that the system is a "way of life" with tenets to guide followers.

The two tenets of judo are Seriyoku-Zen'yo ("Maximum Efficiency with Minimum Effort") and Jita-Kyoei ("Mutual Welfare, Mutual Benefit"). The overall goal of judo, Dr. Kano once said, was to enable individuals to make positive contributions to their societies.

As with many sensei ("instructors"), I am the first to admit that I usually learn more than I teach to a talented group of judoka ("students of Judo"). Usually I pick up a new series of techniques or refine a specific technique that one of the members has perfected. However, one Monday night in December of 1996, I had a major awakening.

As I stood watching the members practice, I realized that many different nationalities and cultures were at work in front of me. I watched a Swahili-speaking member of the 1996 Zaire Olympic Team interrupt the honing of his black belt international competition techniques to help a ten-year-old yellow-belted Vietnamese boy work on his beginner's hip throw. About ten yards away, a green-belted Korean was showing a white-belted Japanese man how to unbalance an opponent for a shoulder throw. An American girl with a brown belt was showing a black American man how to perform a beautiful sacrifice throw. And a few feet away from me, a green-belted muscular

Puerto Rican male was talking quietly in Spanish to an eight-year-old boy, a beginner from Columbia. In some cases, the two judoka did not share a common verbal language; they used motions and the rudimentary Japanese names of techniques to communicate.

My epiphany shook my world: As long as there is a common goal, then all people can unselfishly work toward attainment. Each of these judoka knew that the knowledge they had been given needed to be passed on, and to do so they increased their abilities and stepped closer to their goals of becoming black belts in the future. They knew that they will be judged not by their nationality or color, but by their ability and commitment to their art. Nobody will give them anything in this dojo; they will have to earn it as each black belt before them had done. Nor did they request favors due to color, disabilities, or other factors beyond control; to do so would be to admit defeat before trying.

Perhaps that is what Kano meant when he spoke of individuals making positive contributions to society. As long as the goals are common to all and of equal benefit, then different people can work together to accomplish miracles. Until we as a society realize that to promote or degrade any person due to a factor beyond their control, we are doomed to repeat the errors that seem to erupt periodically in the world. Like the race issue.

When a black belt bows off the mat at the end of each session, it is a local tradition for them to make a comment. I used to say, "Domo arigato gozaimashita" ("Thank you very much.") Since that night and probably forever more, I will say, "Domo, wakarimasen" ("Thanks, now I understand.")

THE FACES BEFORE ME

Blue round eyes and brown oval ones. Blonde straight hair and black kinky hair. Faces of children, adults, and those of the awkward age between. Dressed in white gis, they've all come to learn from me. White, black, and tan faces.

What a terrible responsibility given to me. How can I possibly teach them? From third graders to lawyers, from house painters to housewives, what can I possibly offer them?

Wisdom. What can I tell them? It comes from doing every action as if you will be judged later. Even the little things need to be done morally correct. That is the true nature of personal growth; to act with moral character is to acquire wisdom. Will they believe me?

Desire. The desire is plain on their faces; they want what I have. But there is no secret; my progress came from constant practice. "Never miss practice" worked for me as it had for others. How can I tell them that such a simple method works miracles?

Respect. It surprises me when they treat me with respect. They act as if I have accomplished something that they still pursue. But I still learn. I have not stopped learning. I believe that to stop learning is to stagnate and not progress towards perfection and enlightenment. But perfection is not possible; it is the progress that is important. Will they accept the fact that I am not perfect and hence not a perfect teacher?

Enlightenment. They look for enlightenment through the perfection of their techniques. But my techniques are far from perfect. My enlightenment has come from within by practicing my techniques countless times. How can I pass that on? How can anyone pretend to be able to pass it on to another? It comes from within and is not something that can be reached recipe-style. Hard work, quiet meditation, and introspection were all needed for me to act with perception and judge my deeds accordingly. How can I help them find their own path? What will I tell them?

Commitment. How can I teach them that persistence is the only way to learn the techniques and understand the way of Budo? To fail many times is the norm but to keep coming back until you succeed is the only way to truly know the technique and yourself. How can I help them to learn commitment?

I stand to face them tonight. How will they judge me? What will I teach and what will they learn? Can I teach them to think and act from within?

Will I be a sensei tonight?

LEGACIES: HOPING FOR THE FUTURE WHILE REMEMBERING THE PAST

Human mortality can be a distressing concept to ponder. We are all dying, one day at a time. Some of us have more days than others, but those remaining days are finite in number for us all. Our only hope is that enough days are left so that we can make a legacy that will remain after our final day is done.

Most of us are not fortunate enough to be able to leave a lasting legacy in our occupations. Too many portions of our jobs are beyond our control; few of us are given complete authority. But many of us will find ways to leave a legacy in those things in which we hold true passion. Children, hobbies, charitable causes, and social action are areas in which many of us continue to endeavor to leave a small mark of immortality that will remain after we are gone. For many of us, our jobs are just our livelihoods, they are not our life. Our lives are defined by our passions.

A major portion of my life has been practicing and teaching the martial arts of Judo and Ju-Jutsu. In both arts, the teachers are called "sensei" and it is an honor to be cherished. And feared. Senseis are held to a much higher level than others; perfection in all aspects is considered normal when one speaks about a sensei. It is a position of leadership that truly must pilot by example and enlightenment.

I started my studies in 1974 and have been gifted with the guidance of many fine senseis over the years. As I have progressed, I was called to teach and it has given me a great respect for those martial artists that I call sensei. When I inevitably compare my teaching with theirs, I always fear that I have failed to fulfill the measure they attained.

The secrets of any martial art whisper themselves only to the individual, they cannot be taught en masse like a school subject. Each person moves along the learning path at different rates and times, appropriate for that person at that point in their studies. My greatest challenge is teaching children in the martial arts. Too much or too little knowledge hampers the student's true progress. A great sensei must know how much is sufficient to encourage learning, in both adults and children, without overwhelming the student.

Serious Spencer is one of those great senseis. He leads a Tae Kwon Do club in Charlotte and to watch him instruct is always insightful. Most adults are self-motivated, but children need constant encouragement, praise, and support. Spencer-Sensei imparts these qualities with a genuine concern for his students. In turn, his students give him their highest respect. Our two clubs were cross-training one evening when, at the end of his children's session, he made each child face him and tell him their respective school grades. No matter what answers the child gave, this six-foot tall, two hundred pound, solid-as-a-brick, fifth degree black belt gave each of them a hug and personal words of encouragement. I could see the awe in many of their faces, awe that somebody outside their immediate family cared enough about them to show such concern about their school performance. This awe would project years into their future lives; their sensei was showing them that he had faith in their abilities.

That example was not lost on me. Senseis come in many shapes and a Tae Kwon Do black belt had just taught me a valuable lesson. My apprehension in teaching children was due to one of the most dominating foes in martial arts - fear. This fear, however, came from within me. It was a lack of faith in my ability to teach children. The resulting self-examination also gave me a unique glimpse in how to become a better teacher for all of the members of our club, not just the children. I could stop worrying about the amount of information; even the child could see the destination. They needed help with the journey; help to be shown where they are along that path, help to conquer their internal fears.

Any long-term martial art student will tell you that fear is a natural and common emotion that has kept humans alive for many years. Most of us will tell you that courage is fear that has said its prayers and is determined to accomplish the task, no matter what the cost. It is normal to be scared, just don't stop until you succeed. A sensei should impart that gleaned wisdom when appropriate, telling people to have faith in themselves because the sensei has faith in them, knowing they can perform the task or technique.

I am not as tall or as imposing as Spencer-Sensei, but I hope they understand it, too, comes from my heart. And I hope each of my friends will remember my faith in them as they take their separate journeys.

Many fine sensei have taught me throughout the years. I don't physically see many of them anymore but I recognize their footprints leading down my path in the martial arts. As a sensei, I know that my students are at different locations on the path behind me. My small feet can never fill the giant footsteps of those great senseis in front of me. The best I can do is to plant my foot squarely in their footprints to leave a fresh impression of my own to guide my friends when they reach this place.

The presence of my past senseis resonates faintly with each of my footfalls on that path. Cheatem, Rassmussen, Szrejter, Cates, Fitzgerald, Dewey, Porter, and now Spencer, have blazed bearings to guide me on my journey. And to those sensei in front of me, I say, "Domo, wakarimasen" ("Thanks, now I understand.")

May you all be gifted with such guidance as you leave your legacies.

SATORI AND THE ODD KID OUT

Satori is the Japanese term for a profound insight into a universal truth. It occurs when the recipient listens without prejudice and looks without preconceived notions. In Judo and Ju-Jitsu, it usually comes after many hours of sweat. Only small glimpses are normally earned. On and off the mat, many good ideas can reveal themselves. On a rare occasion, so can a black belt.

Martial Arts camps and seminars are held often during the year to further student's knowledge and studies in the combative ways. There are multiple sessions every day, making for long workouts. A major benefit of attendance is the chance for black belts to talk. One hot summer night in 1996, 50 Judoka (students of Judo) went to a restaurant for food and fellowship.

That night I found myself sitting next to another black belt from my city. He is a weight lifter with balding gray hair. Although we teach in the same area, we never talk socially. Too much to do and too little time, I suppose. I asked him how life was treating him. His answer was surprising

He told me his life is, and always had been, miserable. A failed marriage, too many unfulfilling jobs, and recent legal troubles had not been good to him. The string of misfortunes had followed him into his adult life. He cannot shake the adversity. Judo, he said, is the only constant good thing that he can rely on. Everything else eventually turns bad.

His problems came from being an "odd kid out" as a child. Overweight and with few friends, his childhood had not been pleasant. Choices made as a child have influenced his poor social choices later in life. It is a wisdom spoken from the experience gained from past mistakes. He admits personal responsibility; he alone was responsible for his actions. He has no need to be forgiven. However, if an adult role model had been around, things might have been better.

He now targets the "odd kid out" when they come into his dojo. The other black belts can handle the normal kids and the jocks. When he sees a kid with thick glasses, overweight, or too many freckles, he helps them. Any oddity that makes a kid unsure will draw this black belt closer.

He is not there to be their parent, he said. He doesn't want to be their friend, either. No, he wants to be their ally. He will get on their case when needed, or show encouragement when warranted. He will tell them that, in spite of their differences, they can make it anyway. He will stand with them to show them how to make it. It is up to the "odd kid out" alone to take the initiative. He wants to make them work harder than the normal kids. Acceptance of oneself, including the perceived flaws, will help them face their personal demons.

He confides in a hope for their future, taking responsibility for both his tomorrow and those of the willing "odd kid out." He had faced, and in some personal measure, beaten his own demons. He knows the way if these kids will follow him.

It is a life lesson that is best learned early - early enough to prevent school violence, juvenile delinquency, or taking other paths leading to the rough edge of life. These kids are off society's center and he is encouraging them to influence their own destinies. He wants the "odd kids out" to become better people rather than social outcasts. They can grow up to be isolated from people, causing more problems for themselves and others. The worse cases become killers, unable to judge their actions by our common standards.

A recent success had stoked his fire. He was invited to a nine-year old's birthday party, one of the "odd kids out" that he had helped. He went and spent the afternoon with a bunch of kids. He hit his chest as he said that it got to him. A nine-year-old kid wanted him to be at a party. Him! It really made an impression.

He turned to talk to someone else and did not see me grin. I could see him sitting with a bunch of nine year olds; wearing a ridiculous hat that was too small for him, in a seat with both knees in the air. A fireplug of a middle-aged man with a bunch of little kids.

He was still the "odd kid out," even after all these years. But he had grown from the experience. Now he wanted to help the other "odd kids out." He offers them, and me, a glimpse at a satori that took him years to learn at a terrible cost. He is pointing to a shortcut on some of life's cruelest streets, a bypass to minimize the hard road ahead of them.

And he was rewarded at the party of a grateful nine year old. These are the satori that makes this older "odd kid out" a wealthy soul.

ENJOYING THE PRESENT WHILE LOOKING AT THE FUTURE

A main precept of Zen is to live in the moment. You should learn to enjoy the small things that life sends towards you and not project into the future to look for non-existent problems. I had a similar experience but it allowed me to look to the future with much hope.

Dan and Don joined our Dojo in 1998. Two Vietnamese children, they worked out with us when we were still a club at a local YWCA. Don, the older brother, was fourteen years old and Dan was eleven. Their family had immigrated to the United States and settled in Charlotte, opening a restaurant.

Both brothers worked hard and were accepted by the group. In 2000, Don asked me to write him a letter of recommendation for admittance to Wake Forest University. It was an easy letter to write, as I was impressed with both brother's work ethics and commitment to the martial arts.

Don was accepted to Wake Forest with a full academic scholarship and left Charlotte. Younger Dan would return to our new Dojo to become one of our best Sampais (Senior Students) and an excellent children's instructor. Their mother would keep me informed of Don's progress at college.

Don would return to the Dojo occasionally during the summer months when he was not working. He was taking advantage of his scholarship and studying. Younger brother Dan had become an accomplished martial artist and their bouts were never a sure bet anymore.

One night Don stopped by the Dojo for a brief visit. I was taken aback as I saw a confident young man standing in front of me. The face still bore a resemblance to the wiry young kid, but the person was now an adult. He told me that he was entering his senior year at Wake Forest and was anticipating graduating magna com laude with the hope of entering law school at a prestigious university. Any school would be foolish not to accept him.

Younger Dan was not at the Dojo. He was studying in his SAT course, preparing for that important test. I have no doubt that Dan will also do well in life as his older brother Don.

We never know what life will place in front of us. All of my success and failures have combined to make me the person that I see in the mirror each day. I believe that each person has some control over his/her destiny by building on success and failures. One is just as important as the other.

As Don was leaving the Dojo, I told him that I was proud of his accomplishments and wished him luck in law school. His life is ahead of him with many turns and hills that he cannot possibly see right now. But, he will navigate them well with his good character and work ethic to guide him. I smiled as I enjoyed the moment. I will take no credit for his success; that belongs to Don and his parents. I will, however, take great joy in knowing this outstanding young man.

I also took great joy in knowing that younger Dan was not at the Dojo but studying for his SAT test. His priorities are also in the right place now in his young life.

So for a brief period of time, I enjoyed the moment while looking at a bright future for two friends. A great reward, no matter who you are.

Domo, wakarimasen. (Thanks, now I understand).

THAT KID

Every dojo has one. That kid who never seems to get it. No matter how much personal attention a sensei gives that kid, the techniques are never quite complete and the efforts never seem sincere. Eventually, that kid will wander off to the side, alone and content to not participate. The sensei will continue to help the rest of the children. But that kid sits alone, watching.

Every sensei has tried to help that kid. Many great efforts to make that kid feel as part of the dojo have failed. That kid just won't make the effort. Some senseis have given up, deciding that kid won't be around much longer anyway. Best to give the efforts to those children who want to participate and learn. It's too much of a waste of effort to spend time with that kid alone. Soon that kid is labeled as a failure so no one tries to help anymore.

However, some sensei march to the beat of a different drum. Like trying to punch ice sickles through a concrete wall, they're determined to show that kid the truth no matter who gets hurt. Immovable objects meeting the irresistible force, these sensei try different approaches and offer individual solutions. A few of these senseis become fanatical in their attempts to help that kid. The other senseis shake their heads and walk away, eager to help the good children. The fanatical sensei is determined to show that kid the martial fire. Eager to make that kid a fanatical believer.

At the end of the work-out, the fanatical sensei sits exhausted. Back against the wall and drenched in sweat, the fanatical sensei is reviewing teaching failures. Wanting to know what approaches failed with that kid. As the children leave the dojo, that kid lags behind as always. Finally leaving the dojo, that kid walks by and expresses thanks to the exhausted fanatical sensei. The extra effort, that kid says, helped.

There that kid goes - pants too long and jacket sliding down, the yellow belt dragging behind - trying to catch up with the rest of the children. The fanatical sensei savors the brief moment of success, knowing that both of their martial fires burn a little brighter now. They have given each other a reason to show up the next time; the fanatical sensei and that kid.

www.ingramcontent.com/pod-product-compliance
Lightning Source LLC
Chambersburg PA
CBHW060420090426
42734CB00011B/2389